And Some Are
Walked Home

And Some Are Walked Home

Stories of Grace

LINDA QUANSTROM

Beacon Hill Press of Kansas City
Kansas City, Missouri

Copyright 1994
by Beacon Hill Press of Kansas City

ISBN: 083-411-478X

Printed in the
United States of America

Cover design: Paul Franitza

10   9   8   7   6   5   4   3   2   1

To Judy, who showed me the door;
to Laura, who helped me open it

CONTENTS

INTRODUCTION

You're a Sunday School teacher, and you're looking for a way to introduce a study on the Book of Luke that will be new and fresh and something your longtime, conscientious class hasn't already heard a hundred times. You're a mother of two boys, one 11, one 5, and you're scanning yards of library shelves, trying to find stories for that cross-country automobile trip—stories that will interest the younger one and not bore the older one.

You're a pastor preparing for a board retreat in which you hope two of your lay leaders will be moved to reconcile for the sake of a larger vision. You're a youth pastor, and you're trying to find a way to present the story of Zacchaeus that says more than that he was a short man who climbed a tree to see Jesus. Or perhaps you're an assembly-line worker who's just trying to figure out what grace is all about.

Would you permit me to suggest that this book might be what you're looking for? "And how could one book fit so many different contexts?" you might ask. The key lies in that wonderful, mysterious phenomenon we call story.

It is not happenstance that Jesus told stories to such a wide variety of people in so many different contexts. The crowds who gathered included learned scribes, illiterate fishermen, busy merchants, weary mothers, energetic young people, and wizened grandfathers—all held in rapt attention by His teaching and ministry. And so often the writers of the Gospels record that following His stories, miracles, and redemptive encounters, the people "were amazed."

Amazed.

I grew up in the church. I read about the woman at the well and blind Bartimaeus, and I knew all about short Zacchaeus and his sycamore tree. Wasn't it wonderful what Jesus did for them? I'd think. But what do they have to do with me? I'd wonder. I could relate to the woman who looked for her lost coin and the shepherd who scoured the countryside for his lost lamb. Hadn't I done the same when I'd torn the house apart, looking for my checkbook?

But amazed? No, I was not amazed.

And then it occurred to me to ask myself why. Why did these stories not amaze me? Why didn't they strike me in the face as I was told they did those people who first heard them? There must be more to them than that which surfaced in most Bible story books and Sunday School lessons. There must be aspects to these compact, apparently simple plots and seemingly one-dimensional characters that didn't meet my eye or the eye of just about everyone else who shared the pew with me.

So I decided to try to excavate, if you will, the context and nuances that shaped these stories. I wanted to find out why they caused such a stir when they first sprang from the mind and heart of the Son of God as He spoke from grassy knolls and walked in dusty marketplaces.

The effort helped, to be sure. But analysis didn't necessarily elicit amazement.

It was then that I realized these ancient stories needed to be "explained," not as dissected text, but as stories. These amazing messages needed to be conveyed via the same medium that had carried them so many years ago. They needed to be told as stories in modern equivalent.

The stories in this book are reflections on the Scripture we know so well and the grace of which it speaks. These reflections focus on a series of parables and events relayed in the Gospels that speak directly to the issue of grace.

So I offer this book not as an attempt to re-recite these familiar stories, but as an avenue through which to enter into the power and heat and stunning love that embraced shepherds and scribes, sinners and clergy, old men and young girls, and moved them to mouth-gaping amazement.

Audacious, I know. But I so need to be amazed—grace-amazed. I don't think I'm alone.

1

The Invitation

LUKE 14:15-33

*S*he heard the double <u>slap</u> of the mail slot, followed by the familiar *rish* of paper against hardwood floor, and she rose to <u>retrieve</u> the mail. At first all she saw was a disappointing <u>array</u> of fast-food flyers, but then from the <u>fold</u> of the weekly advertiser fell a square, rag-bond envelope. She picked it up, turned it over, and noticed immediately how beautiful her name looked in <u>calligraphy</u>. She wished she could make her signature <u>curve</u> and <u>slant</u> like that. As she walked to her desk for the letter opener, she looked at the return address. She stood by her desk for several seconds and regarded the invitation; then she laid it square in the middle of the desk at the base of the lamp.

A few blocks away, a man snapped shut his post office box. As he <u>strode</u> toward his car, he quickly <u>shuffled</u> each piece to the bottom of the <u>stack</u> as he skimmed the returns. After he got the square, rag-bond envelope, he stopped. He slowly pulled his keys from his pocket, unlocked the car door, and got in. He put the mail on the seat, turned the key, and drove to his office. When he parked the car and opened the door to leave, he gathered together the assorted letters, catalogs, and bills, but he placed the square, rag-bond envelope on the console between the seats, heaved himself out from behind the wheel, shut and locked the door, and walked into his office.

Across the street from the man's office, a young couple sauntered into the vestibule of their apartment building, arm in arm, laughing. They peered through the small window of their mailbox, knowing that if they found anything at all, it would be some announcement from the manager about laundry room hours. But when they peered through the small window, they saw the end of a white envelope angled across the scratch-clouded glass. They spun the dial of the lock and pulled out a square, rag-bond envelope. They each looked at the return and then at each other. They shut the mailbox door, turned, and walked up the stairs to their apartment, where, once inside, they tacked the envelope on the bulletin board above the kitchen phone.

Several miles away, on a large estate, a gentleman stood in the great hall of his house and rubbed his hands together in anticipation as he surveyed the tables. Each was dressed with Irish linen tablecloths and place settings of silver, crystal, and bone china. The massive buffet table along the long north wall bore an opulent feast. The expectant host smiled as he regarded the baskets of apples, oranges, and bananas, and the platters of avocado, squash, and pumpkin. He watched the steam curl up from lean, red prime rib and the pink moist meat of the coho salmon. He savored the aroma of the fresh breads, pastries, and cakes. All was ready. He walked to the front of his house, swung wide the beveled-glass double doors, and prepared to welcome his guests.

But no one came.

He waited for a long time, pacing on the mosaic tile of

the entry, looking down the long, poplar-lined drive, expecting, any minute, to see the faces of his invited guests. But no one came.

He called his butler and instructed him to telephone the guests and remind them that the dinner to which they had been invited was now ready—the dinner that, when he first mentioned it to them, they all said they wanted to attend.

* * *

She was studying the warranty deed when the telephone rang, and she jumped at the sound of it. Before it rang a second time, she picked it up. The dinner! She ran her fingers across the engraving on the rag-bond card that sat on her desk. Oh yes, she had gotten her invitation, which, by the way, she appreciated very, very much; it was beautifully done, but she was so very sorry—she wasn't going to be able to attend after all. She had just purchased a house and she was preparing to go see it. Please relay her regrets as well as her appreciation to the very thoughtful host. She would love to come another time.

Down the street a few blocks away, the man's secretary, who was obviously not pleased to be working so late, informed him of the call, and he punched the blinking button on his telephone. Yes, this was he. Oh, yes, yes—he did recall receiving the invitation. He put the telephone receiver under his jaw and shuffled through the papers on his desk. Was that tonight? How unfortunate! He had had every intention of coming, but as it turned out, the timing was very bad. Some important, unavoidable business that required his immediate attention had emerged, and he was going to have to beg off. He had just acquired a new company and had to find out what they manufactured. You know how these things are. But please, keep him in mind for the next occasion.

The man and woman raced each other to the telephone and fell into an embrace on the couch, each laughing as the man extended his hand over his wife's shoulder and pulled the receiver to his ear. "I'm sorry, what was that again? Dinner?" He shot a questioning glance at his wife, who motioned toward the kitchen wall. "Oh, yes, yes—I remember now. My, how time flies! I was sure that was next week. Listen—I'm terribly sorry, but you see, I've just gotten married, and . . . well, I . . . um . . . I hadn't had a chance to discuss this with my wife, so I think we're going to have to arrange for a rain check. Have to adjust to new priorities now, you know. But say, it was sure nice to get the invitation."

Disappointment and pain were the first things the butler noticed in the eyes of the host—and then anger. It was anger that rose up, hot and dark red. He shut the double doors, turned away toward the great hall, and then stopped, turned around to the butler, and said, "Call the chauffeur, take the limousine, and go out into the city and invite anyone you see. If those who know me will not come, then I will invite others to come and enjoy my banquet with me."

The butler returned, and within a short time a group of people who received the invitation and set aside their involvements in favor of the host's banquet arrived at the door, were welcomed into the house, and entered the great hall. When empty places still remained, the host sent his servant out again, this time to compel travelers on the highways and visitors from other surrounding cities to join with him and his new friends in the fellowship and nourishment of his great feast.

And when all who wanted to had responded to the invitation, the host closed the heavy beveled-glass doors and entered the great hall to share the abundance of his lavish table, leaving to themselves those who preferred the company of their possessions and affairs and families.

Each one of us has received a personal, grace-wrapped invitation from God to enter into a banquet of abundant fellowship and fulfilling obedience. We are all responsible and engaged people. We have possessions to maintain, obligations to fulfill, and families to nurture. But the invitation has been spoken and must be answered. Will we plead to be excused, or will we forsake all to dine with Him?

Jesus stands on Wall Street today and cries out:

"If anyone comes to Me, and does not hate his own father and mother and wife and children and brothers and sisters, yes, and even his own life, he cannot be My disciple. . . .

"For which one of you, when you want to build a house, does not first sit down and calculate the cost, to see if you have enough to complete it? Otherwise, when you have laid a foundation, and are not able to finish the house, all who observe it begin to ridicule you . . .

"Or what stockholder, when he seeks to take control of a company, does not first sit down and take counsel whether he has proxies enough to seize from the chief stockholder her majority? Or else, while he is in the middle of the vote, he must yield.

"So, therefore, no one who does not give up all can be one of my disciples."*

• • • LUKE 14:15-24 • • •

And when one of those who were reclining at the table with Him heard this, he said to Him,

---

*Author's paraphrase of Luke 14:26, 28-29, 31-33.

"Blessed is everyone who shall eat bread in the kingdom of God!"

But He said to him, "A certain man was giving a big dinner, and he invited many; and at the dinner hour he sent his slave to say to those who had been invited, 'Come; for everything is ready now.' But they all alike began to make excuses. The first one said to him, 'I have bought a piece of land and I need to go out and look at it; please consider me excused.' And another one said, 'I have bought five yoke of oxen, and I am going to try them out; please consider me excused.' And another one said, 'I have married a wife, and for that reason I cannot come.'

"And the slave came back and reported this to his master. Then the head of the household became angry and said to his slave, 'Go out at once into the streets and lanes of the city and bring in here the poor and crippled and blind and lame.' And the slave said, 'Master, what you commanded has been done, and still there is room.' And the master said to the slave, 'Go out into the highways and along the hedges, and compel them to come in, that my house may be filled. For I tell you, none of those men who were invited shall taste of my dinner.'"

2

And Some Are Walked Home

LUKE 15:11-32

*H*e stopped on the road and looked across the lush field of wheat; the gold fingers of the crop curled around the wind, and he thought of the rich soil that had given rise to the splendid yield. He thought of the land, this parcel of land that had given him his name, had given his father his name, and his father before that. As he listened to the rustle of the ripe heads of grain, he thought of this land that had been so wrongfully taken from his father's hand.

He turned away and continued home. He knew what he would see when he rounded the bend. His father would be standing at the edge of the village, hand raised over his eyes, straining to see to the horizon of the road.

The bend in the road had come to represent great pain for this good man. Seeing his father's face, so eager for reunion, watching his father's sorrow-filled vigil, so intent on reconciliation, sliced his heart with more pain than he thought he could bear each time he rounded that bend.

Every day he was reminded of the great disgrace that covered their heads. Every day he was reminded of that one dark day when his unworthy brother had demanded his inheritance—the inheritance that was not yet rightfully his, the inheritance intended for the comforts of his father's old age. The unworthy boy might as well have told his father that he wished him dead. He might as well have killed him.

He remembered how surprised he had been by his father's softness in the face of such insolence. The boy had deserved a lashing, but the old man had stood, silent, holding a long, quiet look into those young, greedy eyes, and then, without a word, he went to his desk, drew out the papers of disposition, and handed the boy the deed to his portion of the land.

This good man was reminded of the shock to all when that unworthy boy actually disposed of the property. Who would have guessed he would do such an unspeakable thing? When he sold that land, he sold his father's retirement—he sold his father's name. He abandoned his father and traded his people, his land, and all he had been taught to hold dear for peoples and lands.

The brother was also reminded of the embarrassment and disgrace he and his father bore in the eyes of their community. To have a reprobate brother was one thing, but to have a father who bowed in the face of such insult and yielded his bounty without thought of recompense was beyond explanation. He felt the disdain of even the children as he passed them in the streets, and he cried in his heart over it.

He had resolved that day, when all they could see of

his younger brother was the back of his head as he rounded the bend, that he would justify the wrong somehow. He would render to his father the service of a faithful, dutiful, good son. He would vigilantly guard what remained of his father's estate. He would make certain that no further disgrace fell upon them.

And so, as he neared the bend in the road, this good man raised his head, straightened his shoulders, and braced himself for the pathetic visage of his father. But when he rounded the bend and could see the wall of the house where his father always waited, he stopped—his father wasn't there. He scanned the walls of the other houses, but the old man was nowhere in sight. The man smiled, almost laughed, and tears came to his eyes as he realized that finally, finally, his tireless work, his careful tending, his unwavering faithfulness had at last redressed the wrong. His father was no longer hungry for the other unworthy son. His father had found nourishment enough to satisfy his loss in the sacrificial service of his good and faithful son.

He didn't quicken his pace as he continued home, for that would have been undignified in such a great moment of justification, but he did step lighter. As he came near to his father's house, he saw men and women scurrying about and children playing in the court. Then he heard music and laughter and thought he heard the clap of dancing inside his father's house. He stopped. He was so overcome with thankfulness that he turned his back to hide his tears of joy. His father was preparing a feast for him. His father was going to honor him for his undaunted devotion and pronounce to all the favor he found in this, his good son.

The smell of roasting meat filled his nostrils, and he could almost taste the succulent beef. He called one of the children over to him and teasingly asked him what occasion it was that prompted this jubilation. The young boy, breathless with excitement, danced from one foot to the other as he said, "Your brother has come, your brother has come. Your father—your father has killed the fatted calf. He's killed the fatted calf because your brother has been received back safe and sound. He's safe and sound."

The man stared at the boy, sure that he was mistaken. He looked up over the boy toward the house. His eyes widened, his heart hammered against his chest, and his fingers clenched into fists—for there, in the doorway of his father's house, was his brother: hair matted, face splotched with grime, wrapped in his father's best robe, shod with new sandals, and honored with nothing less than his father's signet ring.

"You should've seen your father! He was standin' outside the village just like he does every day when suddenly he gave out this shout and started to run. I've never seen a man run before, 'specially not one as rich as your father! His robes were flappin' all around, and he nearly fell once when his foot got caught in his hem.

"We all looked up to see if he'd gone mad, when we saw him fall on this stranger comin' down the road. He hugged him and kissed him and laughed and danced, and almost carried him back to the house. He ordered the servants to dress him in that robe and sandals and to put that ring on his finger, and then they were supposed to kill the fatted calf and invite everyone in the village to celebrate—'cause your father was happy that this son he thought was dead was really alive and that he'd come home."

Every muscle in the man's face tightened. All the blood from his enraged heart pulsed to his cheeks and flushed his skin. His white-knuckled fingers clenched against cold, clammy palms. This was an outrage! All these years he had served his father, he had protected and guarded and cared for him and his estate, he had been prudent and circumspect and good.

And now—this one who had wished their father dead, who had demanded and then squandered their father's retirement, this one who had brought such shame on them by selling and disgracing their name and abandoning them to cavort with sinners, was standing in the doorway of their father's house—wearing their father's robe and sporting the authority of their father's ring. It was madness—nothing but madness!

How could his father be so foolish—so naive? So reckless! So unfair! Surely if there were any justice in the world, he could expect it from his own father. But no, the minute the old man saw the renegade, he abandoned all sense of propriety and decorum and embraced, with undignified, childlike, forgiving enthusiasm, this one who had cost him so much.

What was *he*, then? Where did *he* stand in this disordered scheme of things? What was the worth of all his years of unfaltering service? What was the reward for the agony of his loss, his sacrifice, his embarrassment?

Well, he would have nothing to do with this rash madness. He would not condone it with the blessing of his presence. He would not, he could not, confer the hospitality required of him as the elder brother to family and neighbors who were blatantly ignoring the transgressions of this betrayer, who were covering, as if they were nothing, the stains of his sins with robes and jewels and were sharing with him the meat of the father's riches.

He would not go in. He did not wish to disgrace his father, but perhaps if he refused to perform the customary tribute, he would succeed in bringing his father to reason.

But as he prepared to turn away, he saw his father

hurdle through the doorway, leap past the children, and run to intercept him, breathless, at the end of the road.

"Come, come! Come celebrate! My son, your brother, has come home. Come, my son, come and celebrate. This one I've longed for came seeking to do penance as a servant, but I have forgiven him and have restored him as my child."

"How can you do such a thing? How can you take so lightly what he has done? Look! For all these years I have been serving you, obeying you, I have not once neglected one of your commandments, I didn't demand my inheritance, I didn't leave you, I didn't spend your retirement—and yet you haven't given me so much as a little goat that I might enjoy with my friends. But the minute this immoral, thankless squanderer returns home, you kill the fatted calf and call the whole world to celebrate his return."

"My dear one, you speak as a servant. You are not a servant! You are my beloved child. You know that all I have is yours and has been all these years."

"Yes, but I can't spend any of it until you're dead!"

The words clattered against the silence of the guests, the children, the musicians, and stabbed, like shards of broken glass, the ears of the father. Father and child stood silent in the dusk, father's eyes searching for some glint of softness in the chiseled features of the son.

The father wrapped his hand around the back of the boy's neck and in a low, gentle whisper said, "My son, it is right that we celebrate. It is cause for rejoicing, because this, your brother, was dead but now he has begun to live. He was lost, but now he has been found. Come, come. Don't let jealousy and legalism sour you. Don't clench your fist like a miser and frown like a loveless judge. You are his brother! You are my son! Smile, breathe—leap into my boundless riches. Come, Son. Allow me to embrace you as my child."

We stand at that same bend in the road, and there sweeps down on us an exuberant, embracing grace. We open our mouths to speak. Some of us say, "Father, I am not worthy. Make me a servant." Some of us say, "Father, I am a good servant. Reward me as if I were a loving child."

Some of us allow God to wrap us in His arms of forgiveness, to clothe us in holy array, and to take us into His presence as a beloved and loving child. And some of us stretch forth our arms and hold them stiff against God's chest; we thwart His embrace, we deny and withhold forgiveness, we refuse to participate in His abundance, and we brandish our good works in His face and demand justice.

And some of us are walked home.

• • • LUKE 15:11-32 • • •

And He said, "A certain man had two sons; and the younger of them said to his father, 'Father, give me the share of the estate that falls to me.' And he divided his wealth between them. And not many days later, the younger son gathered everything together and went on a journey into a distant country, and there he squandered his estate with loose living. Now when he had spent everything, a severe famine occurred in that country, and he began to be in need. And he went and attached himself to one of the citizens of that country, and he sent him into his fields to feed swine. And he was longing to fill his stomach with the pods that the swine were eating, and no one was giving anything to him.

"But when he came to his senses, he said, 'How many of my father's hired men have more than enough bread, but I am dying here with hunger! I will get up and go to my father, and will say to him, "Father, I have sinned against heaven, and in your sight; I am no longer worthy to be called your son; make me as one of your hired men."'

"And he got up and came to his father. But while he was still a long way off, his father saw him, and felt compassion for him, and ran and embraced him, and kissed him. And the son said to him, 'Father, I have sinned against heaven and in your sight; I am no longer worthy to be called your son.' But the father said to his slaves, 'Quickly bring out the best robe and put it on him, and put a ring on his hand and sandals on his feet; and bring the fattened calf, kill it, and let us eat and be merry; for this son of mine was dead, and has come to life again; he was lost, and has been found.' And they began to be merry.

"Now his older son was in the field, and when he came and approached the house, he heard music and dancing. And he summoned one of the servants and began inquiring what these things might be. And he said to him, 'Your brother has come, and your father has killed the fattened calf, because he has received him back safe and sound.'

"But he became angry, and was not willing to go in; and his father came out and began entreating him. But he answered and said to his father, 'Look! For so many years I have been serving you, and I have never neglected a command of yours; and yet you have never given me a kid, that I might be merry with my friends; but when this son of yours came, who has devoured your wealth with harlots, you killed the fattened calf for him.' And he said to him, 'My child, you have always been with me, and all that is mine is yours. But we had to be merry and rejoice, for this brother of yours was dead and has begun to live, and was lost and has been found.'"

3

What Hangs in the Balance?

MATT. 18:23-35

*S*ebria, my dear sister,

I suppose you've heard through Gaius what has happened. I know he was going to visit you on his way to Tycor, but I am writing, not to further burden you with concern, but to try to find some relief to my great sorrow. You've always known how to comfort me, and even though you are far away, I can see your gentle eyes and know, as I sit here and write to you, that your love is with me now.

Where do I begin? It was all so sudden—so inconceivable. Just seven days ago my life was safe and happy. Now, as if in a blinking of an eye, it is dark and void of hope. All its light has been sucked out.

I suppose the seeds for this present trouble started years ago. When Jerome came to work for the king, we felt so blessed, as you know. I mean, so many less-inviting things could have happened, but here we were, among the servers of the king. And Jerome did so well. He was promoted so many times those first two years we would laugh about the air getting so thin we couldn't catch our breath. The children were all healthy and happy, and although I missed you dearly, I enjoyed the company of some wonderful friends.

What I find so strange is that I had no hint of the things that lurked behind Jerome's smiling face. You'd think, if you live with a man for 12 years and have five children by him, that you'd be able to tell if something were amiss. But I tell you, Sebria, I did not know. I truly didn't. Now that I reflect back, I can see things that might have given me clues, of course, but at the time they were of no consequence. It's only now that I see them in their true significance.

As I was saying, Jerome had won the confidence of the king and was given charge of the king's private holdings. He managed his properties and his investments and even the queen's checkbook. There was some jealousy on the part of his colleagues, of course, but on the whole, Jerome was respected by all—or so I thought.

It wasn't until we received the summons that I understood that things were not as they seemed. Oh, Jerome had been short-tempered recently, but he'd had similar spells off and on, and since they never amounted to much, I paid them little attention. But, as I said, we received a summons to appear before the king.

Well, you can imagine what I thought! Jerome had done so well, and since the king was such a generous person, I thought he was going to bestow some honor on Jerome and wanted all of us to be able to share in the celebration. What a fool I was, Sebria! What a fool I am!

I thought it was peculiar that Jerome was so tense, in

light of this pending good fortune, but I didn't give it too much thought. I was more concerned with what to wear and if the children would behave properly. Such a stern lecture I gave them! Oh, my poor babies—my poor babies!

Well, we managed to get ourselves ready. I was a little put out that the king hadn't given us more notice. Three hours is hardly enough for a family of seven. And we still have only the one bathroom. But we managed somehow and made our way to court.

Oh, Sebria, it is such a splendid place. I'd had only the one glance of it that first year we were here, and I'd thought my memory had exaggerated it, but no, it was grander even than I'd remembered. The pink marble and great stones and the gold and silver—it's just too much to take in. I can't begin to describe it to you. Just setting foot in the doorway sends shivers down your back, and you're stuck immediately with the sense of smallness.

Just as we'd passed through the door, an officer met us, and Jerome motioned for me to follow the man, so the children and I followed him over to the side of the great hall and walked along the wall behind the pillars toward the throne. Jerome was led straight up the middle of the hall. I could hear his footsteps echo smartly off the floor. He walked so straight and looked so dignified. I was so proud of him—oh, I was so proud of him!

The officer stopped suddenly, and poor little Tychius walked right into the back of the man's leg. The soldier didn't move, but I could tell he wasn't pleased. I pulled little Tychius next to me, and we turned to watch. The king motioned for Jerome to step forward, which he did. Then the king spoke to a man who was standing next to the throne. He looked like a scribe or scholar or something like that. The man held up a long parchment and started to read.

"Jerome of Tycor." Dear Sebria, I must admit, tears

came to my eyes—I was so overcome with pride. Knowing from what humble circumstances this dear man of mine had come, and to stand there with his children and be able to hear this great announcement of honor from someone so wise as the king—well, it was simply overwhelming. The man's voice bounced from every pillar as he read the decree, ". . . servant of the king these 12 years and overseer of all his houses and lands these 7 years, you are found guilty of gross negligence and fraud and disregard for our great king through deceit, and having accrued a debt to the king of $2.3 million, you are hereby charged to be sold, along with your wife and all your children, and all that you own in repayment to the king and his household."

Sebria, the words shot like a flaming catapult through my heart, which turned to ice on my spine. I could not believe my ears. I looked at the scribe and then at the king, sure I would see some glint of good humor. Surely this was a joke. They could not be serious! My Jerome, my hardworking, diligent Jerome, negligent? Fraudulent? No! No! It's a lie! It's a lie! The soldier moved suddenly, and I realized I was screaming out loud. I bit my lip and gathered in the children. They gripped my hands and thighs. Their little hands were cold. I knew I couldn't cry. I had to be strong. I had to somehow show these people how wrong they were. I had to believe they were wrong.

Ten million dollars, Sebria—$10 million! I didn't know there was that much money in the whole world; how could one man be in debt for $10 million? We were comfortable, but not by any means wealthy. Our house is modest, and I don't own more than three dresses. What could Jerome have done with $10 million? It was preposterous.

I looked up to try to see his face, but he was gone. I stopped breathing. And then I heard him. He was crying, and he was facedown before the feet of the king. His arms were stretched out above his head, and his hands were clasped tightly, trembling, as he pleaded with the king: "Your Grace, please have patience with me, please have patience with me. I will repay everything. I will repay everything." I was horrified. It was true! Jerome owed the king $10 million.

This man I thought I knew, this man I loved, had squandered or stolen or lost—I don't know which—more money than all the heavens contain. And he was promising to pay it all back. It was impossible. Never could he repay that money—never. And our family was going to be torn from each other and sold as slaves. My babies! My babies! Oh, Sebria, I couldn't help myself; I sank to my knees and sobbed. The children were frightened and were crying, but even as they were crying they were trying to comfort me. I grabbed them in to me and clung to them. No one was going to take my babies—no one.

Then it happened. Even before Jerome had taken a breath, the king stood and walked down the steps to him. Was he going to kill him there and then? He bent over, took Jerome by the arms, raised him up, and said to him, "You are forgiven your debt, Jerome. I forgive you your debt."

I waited, not sure I understood, but then the king smiled and told him to take his family and go. I sobbed and laughed and kissed the heads of each of my children. Jerome came over, pulled me to my feet, and we walked quickly past the pink pillars and out into the sunshine. We walked out of that grand court, released of our debt.

Sebria, my dear, dear sister. I will never, so long as I live, be able to tell you the nature of the joy I felt or the depth of my gratitude for the king. He spared us! He had every right to sell us, our children, and all we owned to try to recover that which Jerome had squandered, but instead, he forgave us. He simply forgave us. He canceled the debt! That inconceivable, unfathomable debt—forgiven. I tell you, Sebria, I would have done anything for that king—anything. No sacrifice and no effort would have been too great.

But I will never understand Jerome as long as I live. How he could do what he did after having received such mercy I will just never understand. We had just turned the corner onto our street when he sprang away from me and lunged toward a man coming toward us. He gripped the man by the throat and screamed at him, "Pay back what you owe me! Pay back what you owe me!" The man pleaded with Jerome to have patience with him, that he'd pay the $100 back, that he just needed a little patience.

Two men intervened and wrestled Jerome off the man, and so I herded the children into the house and slammed the door. I was so angry with Jerome I was beside myself. I tell you, Sebria, if he'd come through that door I think I would have hit him flat out with a skillet. How could he be so base in light of what had just happened? Who was this father of my children? What had happened to him? What? To be forgiven so much and then not to forgive. I mean, the man owed him only pennies compared to what Jerome owed the king. Pennies! Through his own carelessness he had put himself and his family in grave jeopardy, and then, when all was done, he turns on a poor man owing him pennies.

Well, Jerome didn't come home until well into the night. I think he knew he wouldn't be welcomed. I don't know if he was trying to save his ego or what, but he boasted about throwing the poor man into prison. That was more than I could take, Sebria—it was simply too much. I decided not to say a word to him, because if I got started, I didn't know where I'd stop. So I told him dinner was in the refrigerator, and I went to bed.

Well, the next day came a second summons from the king. Jerome never came home. The king threw him into prison. I understand the king was incensed, as well he should be, that Jerome did not show mercy when so much mercy had been afforded him.

I don't known what will become of us. I can't think. I can't cry. I know the tears will come, because I do love him. But you know, I don't know if my sorrow is greater for having lost the one I love or for seeing such evil in the heart of one I thought was so good.

Please write to me, Sebria. I need the comfort of one I know loves me.

All my love, your sister,
Lytia.

* * *

They stood in the shadow of the crossbeam and looked up and laughed at the Man stained with blood and spittle. The cloudless blue sky turned a heavy gray purple, and the wind blew cold. A spasm clenched the Man's right arm and jerked the flesh of His hand against the spike that impaled it. The Man raised His head in agony. He opened His eyes and saw the men clustered in the shadows sneering at Him—and behind them, the faces of all the men and women and children yet to be. He threw back His head, inhaled as much breath as He could, and, looking down at His mockers, said, "Father, forgive them, for they do not know what they are doing."

And then the wind stopped, and all sound was sucked from the air. "Father, into Thy hands I commit My spirit."

Black blotched the purple sky, the ground heaved and shuddered, and rocks and sepulchers cracked and crumbled. A volcanic clap as of the primeval renting of land from firmament ruptured the heavens as the Logos, the very

Thought and Word of the eternal high and holy God, was ripped and crushed by the teeth of death, and the beloved Son, God from God, died, the debt of sin to pay. When God the Son heaved His last cosmic-rendering sigh, and as a sorrow-laden silence descended on Golgotha, forgiving love pulsed, unseen, and kissed the heads of all humanity.

And each blessed person turned; and as they walked away, brothers seized the throats of brothers, daughters their fathers, husbands their wives, and neighbor demanded satisfaction from neighbor.

• • • MATT. 18:23-35 • • •

"The kingdom of heaven may be compared to a certain king who wished to settle accounts with his slaves. And when he had begun to settle them, there was brought to him one who owed him ten thousand talents. But since he did not have the means to repay, his lord commanded him to be sold, along with his wife and children and all that he had, and repayment to be made. The slave therefore falling down, prostrated himself before him, saying, 'Have patience with me, and I will repay you everything.' And the lord of that slave felt compassion and released him and forgave him the debt.

"But that slave went out and found one of his fellow slaves who owed him a hundred denarii; and he seized him and began to choke him, saying, 'Pay back what you owe.' So his fellow slave fell down and began to entreat him, saying, 'Have patience with me and I will repay you.' He was unwilling however, but went and threw him in prison until he should pay back what was owed.

"So when his fellow slaves saw what had happened, they were deeply grieved and came and reported to their lord all that happened. Then summoning him, his lord said to him, 'You wicked slave, I forgave you all that debt because you entreated me. Should you not also have had mercy on your fellow slave, even as I had mercy on you?' And his lord, moved with anger, handed him over to the torturers until he should repay all that was owed him.

"So shall My heavenly Father also do to you, if each of you does not forgive his brother from your heart."

4

The Neighbor
Who Wasn't

LUKE 10:25-37

*T*he blow struck from nowhere.

He heard the snapping crack of wood against bone, and his knees buckled and his hands slapped the ground. Rough fingers pulled and yanked and scratched. They twisted his arms in every direction and struck, with hard blows, the small of his back. His face was shoved hard against the raw, stony road, and his teeth scraped across the suffocating grit.

Then, as suddenly as they had come, they were gone. Gone, along with everything else.

His coat was gone; his suit was in shreds; his money, his identification, and all his cards, with his favorite picture of his daughter—gone. And his briefcase—his briefcase with his manuscript. Oh, not his manuscript!

How could this have happened? His lifework—gone; everything gone. Two minutes ago he had had money and credit. Just two minutes ago he had had Pulitzer prize work in his possession, and he had had a purpose and a mission. Two minutes ago he had had plans and great dreams and the wherewithal to carry them out. Now all he had was nakedness and pain and not strength enough to speak his name.

"O God, let me die. Please let me die."

It was high noon when he awoke. Sweat drenched his forehead and clouded his eyes. He tried to move, but the pain was too great.

Then he heard them—bells. The soft jingle got louder and distinct. "I'm saved. I'm saved. A priest." He tried to call out, but his tongue wouldn't move. He waited. The bells stopped. Silence. When he heard them again, they clanged and jangled in erratic staccato and then faded. Silence.

"No, no. He's gone. How could he leave? How could he . . . he thought I was dead. He thought I was dead. He couldn't touch a dead body. O, God, sometimes Your law is so hard.

"I must move. I must sit up. I must yell out."

A shadow stretched across his face, and he opened his eyes and saw the hem of a Levite's robe. "Oh, just in time. Just in time." He moved his cracked lips, but he couldn't form a word. He tried to turn his head and smile, but his neck froze in a cramp. He waited. Any second he would feel cool water grace his lips—any second.

And then he felt it: heat—white heat. The shadow was gone.

"No! No! This cannot be. It simply cannot be—this is all wrong. This is not how it's supposed to be! All is upside down. Right and order are overthrown. How could a Levite abandon me? He could see I was alive. He *did* see I was alive. He could see I was a brother. He *did* see that I was a brother. If not you, then who? If not you, my brother, then *who?*

"O, God, what have I done to call down such wrath? I am a righteous man. I am a man of position, of substance. I pay my tithes, I stand in the gate, I have a name.

"How is it that I am helpless?

"How is it that I am broken?

"How is it that I am a victim of such evil?

"How is it that I am destined to die?

"Oh, my God, have mercy. Have mercy."

A cool liquid seeped around his skull, and he felt the gentle pulse of cloth against wound.

"Oh, dear One of great mercy, a brother has come. A brother has come." The strong, sure arms turned and straightened his battered body, and he raised his head to meet the quiet gaze of a Samaritan.

Is it not a wondrous thing that the ones most ready and able to embrace our brokenness with solace and comfort are not those who come to us in strength and composure, not the ones with resources and position, but those instead who come to us in pain, marred by indignity, bereaved by loss, or wounded by prejudice and injustice?

Is it not a wondrous thing that when we feel our wounds and recognize our helplessness and realize our destiny with death, when we call the pain searing through our joints for what it is, that in that moment of namelessness there comes to us, not the light of the One high and lifted up, but the tug of a scarred hand and the cleansing balm of water and blood? And is it not a wondrous thing that when we look up, we meet the eyes of One we know understands our pain, and we rest in the arms of the One wounded for our transgressions, the One bruised for our iniquities, the One through whose stripes we are healed?

And is it not indeed a wondrous thing that He says to us, "Go and do the same"?

THE NEIGHBOR WHO WASN'T

• • •   LUKE 10:25-37   • • •

And behold, a certain lawyer stood up and put Him to the test, saying, "Teacher, what shall I do to inherit eternal life?"

And He said to him, "What is written in the Law? How does it read to you?"

And he answered and said, "You shall love the Lord your God with all your heart, and with all your soul, and with all your strength, and with all your mind; and your neighbor as yourself."

And He said to him, "You have answered correctly; do this, and you will live."

But wishing to justify himself, he said to Jesus, "And who is my neighbor?"

Jesus replied and said, "A certain man was going down from Jerusalem to Jericho; and he fell among robbers, and they stripped him and beat him, and went off leaving him half dead. And by chance a certain priest was going down on that road, and when he saw him, he passed by on the other side. And likewise a Levite also, when he came to the place and saw him, passed by on the other side. But a certain Samaritan, who was on a journey, came upon him; and when he saw him, he felt compassion, and came to him, and bandaged up his wounds, pouring oil and wine on them; and he put him on his own beast, and brought him to an inn, and took care of him. And on the next day he took out two denarii and gave them to the innkeeper and said, 'Take care of him; and whatever more you spend, when I return, I will repay you.'

"Which of these three do you think proved to be a neighbor to the man who fell into the robbers' hands?"

And he said, "The one who showed mercy toward him." And Jesus said to him, "Go and do the same."

5

Finders—Keepers; Losers—Weepers

LUKE 15:1-10

*C*aleb knelt to the ground, bent forward, and eased the sheep off his shoulders. Recognizing familiar territory, the animal jerked forward and kicked its hind legs, wrapping one in the folds of Caleb's robe. Both animal and man lost their balance and splatted, facedown to the ground. As the sheep scampered free, Caleb rolled to his back, heaved a relieved sigh, and started to laugh.

Oh, was he tired, so tired, but oh—so, so happy. He and his lost sheep were home.

"Caleb! Caleb!"

Caleb raised himself up on his elbows and looked around to see Joshua running toward him, his robe flapping excitedly in the wind.

"Joshua!"

"Caleb, Caleb—where have you *been? Where *have* you

been? You *missed* Him. You missed *Him!* I tell you—this time He outdid himself. He really did. You'll *never* believe what He said. You'll just never believe it!"

Caleb had rolled over and raised up on his knees and smiled at his beloved friend.

"Joshua! Slow down." Caleb yielded to Joshua's upward pull on his arm and stood to his feet. "What are you talking about?" he asked, shaking the dust from his robe.

Joshua flailed around Caleb, slapping the man's chest, back, and legs with both hands to evict the dust, and with each released puff he blurted out portions of his story.

"You know, you *know* that Man Jesus, that Man *Jesus*— the one who hosted that dinner we were invited to Monday? You know, the One who says all those peculiar things?"

"Joshua! I'm fine; it'll wash. Josh. Stop!"

"Oh, yes—sorry." Joshua pulled one hand to his chest but continued to brush dust from Caleb's shoulder with the other.

"Well, what about Him?"

"Oh, yes. *Yes.* Well, late this morning as we were all listening to Him—He had stopped to answer some of our questions, you see—well, some of those hoity-toity Pharisees started to interrupt and make a do about that dinner, you know, that dinner the other night.

"What about it?" Caleb asked as he coaxed Round-belly into the pen.

"Well, that was just their point! What was Jesus, who's supposed to be this Rabbi, doing hosting a dinner for us low-lifes? Those Pharisees, bless their starched backs, couldn't figure why this here righteous Man would contaminate himself by eating with publicans and tax takers and shepherds and the like."

Caleb hoisted the gate and pushed it shut. "Well, to be honest, Joshua, I wondered about that myself."

"Well, why shouldn't He? Man! I mean, they can get a gnat up their noses same as we can; just 'cause they can parade around in their fine, tinkling robes doesn't have to mean they're better than we are!"

"It's not their clothes that makes them different, Joshua. It's their law keeping."

"But how are we supposed to keep all those laws when we don't even know what they all are? Not fair, Caleb. It's not fair! Never *been* fair. *Never* been fair!"

"Anyway, what happened next?"

"Oh, yeah—that's the good part. He tells them this story—one of those stories He tells all the time—you know, the ones you can't digest, but they leave a taste in your mouth anyway?"

"Yeah."

"Well, this one was clear as the stars at night, Caleb—clear as the stars at night." Joshua leaned toward Caleb and whispered, "He told them they was like shepherds."

Caleb stopped pulling on the leather latch, looked at Joshua, and frowned. "No!"

"Yes. Yes. I mean He didn't say it directlike, but He said it just the same. You should've heard Him, Caleb. You should've heard Him. I mean, there we all were, minding our own business, listening politelike, when these four Pharisees move in and start bad-mouthing that there dinner the other night. Now I know I don't understand all that that Man says, but I know He wasn't talking about any dinner. But these guys—they don't care. They're just mad 'cause He was giving us the time of day and acting like He was one of us, and so they start giving Him trouble about sharing the same table with the likes of us. Well, don't you know things got quiet? Things got *quiet*. I'm surprised those fellows had such nerve, seeing how many of us there were compared to them. Well, what do you think happened, Caleb? What do you think happened?"

Caleb leaned against the gatepost, knowing he was going to get the long version of the story. He rubbed the small of his back against the rough wood and obliged Joshua. "I've no idea, Joshua. What?"

"Well, things are quiet now, you know. All you could hear was my wife. We were in the court outside my house, you see. Well, all you could hear was my wife banging pots and dishes around. We all just waited. Then He said it. He looked them straight in the eyes, and He said, 'What man among you, if he has a hundred sheep . . .' Caleb, you should've seen their faces. You should've seen their faces. They knew He was talking to them, 'cause they was on one side of the crowd, and He wasn't looking at nobody else but them. One guy got so purple you couldn't tell where he ended and his robe began! I thought Jesus was being kinda polite, seeing as He let them have 100 sheep instead of our measly 5 or 10."

Caleb laughed as Joshua paused long enough to wipe the sweat from his brow with the palm of his hand. "But that wasn't the really *good* part, Caleb; that's not the good *part*—I mean, I never!" he said as he ran his wet hand across the front of his ample waist. "I never heard such a story. Jesus says, still looking at these Pharisees, mind you, He says, 'What man among you, if he lost 1 of his 100 sheep . . .' Now this flock isn't goats and sheep, mind you, Caleb; they's all sheep, they's all the same, and He says, '. . . if one of you lost 1 of his sheep, would not leave the 99 in the wilderness and go after the 1 which is lost until he finds it?' Now, that's true—any of us would go get the vagrant, particularly if we had 100. You don't get that many by letting them get lost on you, now, do ya?" As he laughed at his own joke, Joshua took hold of the fence rail and shifted his weight.

"OK," said Caleb, folding his arms across his chest, "this shepherd has 100 sheep, 1 is lost, and of course he'd go look for it, leaving the others with the other shepherd."

"Well, sure, that's what we'd do, but Jesus doesn't say nothing about any other shepherd—that's important."

"OK, that's important. What happens then?"

"Well, when this shepherd finds his sheep, of course it knows it's lost, and so it's just siting there on the ground, bleating like it'll never see another day; and this shepherd, he sees it, hoists it up across his shoulders, 'cause he knows it isn't going to get up and walk on its own, but while he's doing all this, the shepherd is rejoicing."

"Rejoicing?"

"Yeah, that was a part I didn't understand. I mean, we're happy enough to find a lost sheep, but it's enough to kill ya getting them home again. They refuse to walk. They have to be carried, and they weigh a ton. It's perilous work getting them home, but Jesus says that this shepherd is rejoicing all the way home. But that's not the best part."

"OK, I'm listening. Go on."

"Well, when this shepherd gets home, he calls all his friends and neighbors together for a celebration over finding this lost sheep."

"Well, yeah, getting sheep and self back safe and sound is reason enough to celebrate."

"Yes, Caleb, yes, but then Jesus, still looking at these Pharisees, says to them, 'In the same *way*, in the *same* way as the shepherd and all his kind celebrate over reclaiming one lost sheep,' *listen* to this"—Joshua reached forward and gripped Caleb's arm—"listen to *this*: 'in the same way, there will be more joy in heaven over one sinner who repents, than over ninety-nine righteous persons who need no repentance.' Oh, Caleb, you should've *seen* their faces. You should have seen their *faces*! Wowee—I think it was good we all was around Jesus, 'cause I'm not sure they wouldn't have gone off and thrown rocks at Him, they was so mad. Can you believe He *said* that? Can you *believe* it—

that heaven would be happier over just one of us law-breaking sinners repenting than with all them there nice, clean, law-keeping Pharisees?"

Caleb looked through and past the question in his friend's eyes and was silent—that heaven would rejoice more over a repentant sinner than over an assembly of righteous law-keepers. Would heaven rejoice over *him*? Before he or Joshua could say another word, Joshua's wife burst out of her house, hand raised, shouting, "I found it! I found it!"

The two men squinted against the sun to see what she held and could only catch the glint of something shiny.

"I found my coin! I found my coin!" She stretched out her hand to show her neighbor: "This morning I noticed that my dowry necklace was missing one coin, and I looked everywhere. I looked everywhere! I had only the 10. My father sacrificed so much even for those, and I just *had* to find it. I'd never be able to replace it—never. And I *found* it! Oh, we have to have a party. We have to have a party! I found my coin! I found my coin!"

As she bounced up the street, inviting her friends to celebrate, Joshua laughed, relieved he wasn't going to share dinner with a wife with one lost dowry coin, and looked back at his friend.

"Where were you all day, anyway, Caleb? I even came out to the graze land to find you."

"Uh? Oh, I had to go find Round-belly. I was geting ready to move to the north well when I noticed she was gone. I'd just gotten back with her when you saw me."

Joshua slapped his friend on the back, sending a puff of dust into the air. "I guess we'd better have a party! You find your lost sheep, my wife finds her lost coin. Heaven's *singing*, Caleb—I just *know* heaven's singing."

That night, under the black expanse of the star-studded sky, shepherds, and publicans, tax-gatherers, adulterers, liars, gossipers, doubters, vow-breakers, and all the people who recognized their sin ate and danced and celebrated the fellowship and grace of the One named Jesus, the One who found them, embraced them, and rejoiced to call them by name.

And out in the wilderness, under that same sky, sat 99 righteous ones who needed no repentance.

• • • LUKE 15:1-10 • • •

Now all the tax-gatherers and the sinners were coming near Him to listen to Him. And both the Pharisees and the scribes began to grumble, saying, "This man receives sinners and eats with them." And He told them this parable, saying,

"What man among you, if he has a hundred sheep and has lost one of them, does not leave the ninety-nine in the open pasture, and go after the one which is lost, until he finds it? And when he has found it, he lays it on his shoulders, rejoicing. And when he comes home, he calls together his friends and his neighbors, saying to them, 'Rejoice with me, for I have found my sheep which was lost!' 'I tell you that in the same way, there will be more joy in heaven over one sinner who repents, than over ninety-nine righteous persons who need no repentance.

"Or what woman, if she has ten silver coins and loses one coin, does not light a lamp and sweep the house and search carefully until she finds it? And when she has found it, she calls together her friends and neighbors, saying 'Rejoice with me, for I have found the coin which I had lost!' In the same way, I tell you, there is joy in the presence of the angels of God over one sinner who repents."

6

The Cloak of Darkness; the Voice of Light

MARK 10:46-52

*H*e could feel the heat of the sun across his shoulders, and he thought of slipping his great cloak off for a while. But business was good, and if he took off his cloak, they might not take as much notice and might pass him by. So he sat in the hot sun, wrapped in his great cloak, hands cupped out in front, begging mercy to a blind man.

Coins plunked heavily against his palms, and Bartimaeus smiled within himself. Passover was a blessing from God in more ways than one, and the Passover pilgrims traveling today were especially generous—not that things ever got really quiet on this thoroughfare. He was fortunate, and he knew it. If he'd lived in most any other place, he would never have fared so well. Jericho, the great "perfumed city," was the place to live, all right—especially if you were blind or lame.

Caravans of merchants making a fortune in the Damascus-Arabia trade passed in and out of the city every day. Well-fed and satisfied soldiers thanked the city by giving to the beggars whenever leaving to return to their regiments. The tax collectors headquartered here assuaged their guilt with alms, and the priests and Levites commuting to and from Jerusalem satisfied their duty by throwing coins to the unfortunate. They all came to Jericho, the crossroads of one kind of business or another, and they all gave.

Bartimaeus had early learned how to glean a comfortable living from his five-pace piece of the Jericho road. And as he sweated under the weight of the fabric and felt the sticky threads cling to his back, he knew his great cloak played no small part in his success. It told passersby of his occupation and warned other beggars of his station. He wore it by day to draw gifts; he huddled under it in the winter and cushioned his head with it in the summer. He hid the store of his wealth in its faded roan folds.

And today, the accumulation inside his cloak was unusual, even for the week before Passover. The passersby seemed excited and agitated. Their speech was as rushed as their pace. They were talking about something, something unusual, and Bartimaeus tried to shut out the cries of his fellow beggars to listen. He'd learned a great deal about the intrigue of the world over the years. People didn't think blind beggars could hear. And he was eager to learn something new. It was one of the ways to break the monotony and to forget the cramp in his arms.

Things had been rather humdrum of late, and the news had been routine. Not since that time past when that Jesus Prophet had done and said so many astounding things was there such a stir. Bartimaeus had often wondered what would have happened had he known more about this Jesus back then. Would the Man have healed him? And if He had, what would that mean? Oh, more than anything, Bartimaeus wanted to regain his sight. He wanted to see the tall, swaying palms of Jericho. He wanted to see the green stirring of the sweet-smelling balsam. He wanted to know if the roses occasionally thrown to him were red or yellow. But seeing would bring more than motion and color to Bartimaeus. It would bring a different life, and he'd wondered a great deal about that.

He'd been blind a very long time, and he wasn't practiced at any trade other than begging. If he weren't blind, how would he live? What would he do to support himself? He'd have to start over, and as resourceful as he was, Bartimaeus wondered if he'd be able to survive such a new life. But it was idle thought. He didn't know back then what Jesus could do, and now, when he did know, Jesus wasn't here.

Bartimaeus hadn't realized how far his mind had wandered when he was awakened by a sudden surge of movement and sound. Men and women were rushing past him, and children were colliding into him. He could feel the accidental slap of thin arms and legs as children clamored to keep up with their parents. This was more than the usual street greeting given a new caravan. Someone important was coming.

He leaned toward a neighboring beggar: "What is it? Who's coming?"

"Jesus. The Jesus who is the Nazarene."

Bartimaeus' blind eyes widened. His heart started to pound, and his chest pulsed with short, shallow breaths. He jerked his head to listen and determine the direction of the visitor. His mind raced from prospect to fear and back again. It was here—his chance to see. It was slapping him in the face, and he didn't know what to do. Did he want to see and maybe starve, or remain blind and safe, huddled in the warm folds of his cloak? And he had to decide. There was no time to think it through. No time to work out a plan—no time. The crowd pressed in on him. People weren't running by anymore—they were stepping on his feet, falling against his back, standing on the strained drape of his cloak. And they were shouting: "Jesus! Jesus!"

The words rumbled up out of his chest and vaulted into the air before he had time to think: "Jesus, Son of David, have mercy on me! Jesus, Son of David, have mercy on me!" Each plea cut ever sharper through the din of the crowd, and those near him, annoyed by his noise, demanded he be quiet. But Bartimaeus raised to his knees, flailed his arms, and shouted all the more loudly, "Son of David, have mercy on me!"

There was so much noise, and Bartimaeus was so intent on his being heard, that he didn't notice that the rebukes had turned to encouragement. Finally, someone shook his shoulder and shouted in his ear, "Take courage—arise! He is calling for you. He is calling for you."

Bartimaeus jumped to his feet, pulled his cloak from his shoulders, and lunged forward through the crowd. His hands, stretched stiff before him, jabbed the onlookers, and he felt their hands pull and press him forward toward Jesus. Then the movement all stopped, and Bartimaeus' hands met a man's chest and chin. "What do you want Me to do for you?" Bartimaeus could feel the warmth of Jesus' breath, and he curled his fingers around the cloth of Jesus' robe in a childlike grip. "Rabboni, I want to see again. I want to regain my sight!"

He knew when he spoke them that the words plummeted him into unmarked openness. But he flung them before Jesus and eagerly rent the fabric of his safe-and-secure existence.

"Go your way. Your faith has made you well."

Light. Shape. Color. White teeth strung in a smile. Brown skin and dark, warm eyes. Bartimaeus saw the face of Jesus. Bartimaeus could see.

Jesus turned toward the road, and Bartimaeus followed. The people of Jericho disbursed to their houses and markets. And there, by the deserted road, in a dust-layered heap, lay Bartimaeus' great cloak.

• • •   MARK 10:46-52   • • •

Then they came to Jericho. As Jesus and his disciples, together with a large crowd, were leaving the city, a blind man, Bartimaeus (that is, the Son of Timaeus), was sitting by the roadside begging. When he heard that it was Jesus of Nazareth, he began to shout, "Jesus, Son of David, have mercy on me!"

Many rebuked him and told him to be quiet, but he shouted all the more, "Son of David, have mercy on me!"

Jesus stopped and said, "Call him."

So they called to the blind man, "Cheer up! On your feet! He's calling you." Throwing his cloak aside, he jumped to his feet and came to Jesus.

"What do you want me to do for you?" Jesus asked him.

The blind man said, "Rabbi, I want to see."

"Go," said Jesus, "your faith has healed you." Immediately he received his sight and followed Jesus along the road *(NIV)*.

7

What's in a Name?

LUKE 19:1-10

*H*e came out of his house and squinted in the face of the sunlight. He heard the uproar of voices and slap of feet against the hard dirt before he could see what the disturbance was all about. People ran by him; some rammed into his shoulders as they hurried past and jerked him this way and that. As he darted around the heedless bodies and struggled to reach the protection of his doorway, he heard women cry, "Jesus!" "Jesus!" and he heard men, carrying children on their shoulders, shout, "Hurry! Hurry!"

Jesus! That explains it! That Man Jesus was coming. Zacchaeus turned his head in the direction of the crowd's exodus and stretched to see the One they sought. All he could see was dust and the backs of everyone's heads. He jumped and still could see nothing. He didn't believe all the stories he'd heard about this Jesus, but he was curious and wanted to see what He looked like. After all, it wasn't every day that someone came along who could draw shopkeepers and merchants—and tax collectors—away from their money-gathering busyness.

Zacchaeus pursed his lips. How was he going to get a look at this man? Zacchaeus wasn't used to not getting what he wanted. He'd realized while still very young what he could and could not expect out of life, and he'd set his sights early on getting all it did offer. As soon as he was old enough to do so, he channeled his considerable energy, his exuberant determination, from escaping the boys who bullied him to outfoxing them. He would not be victimized! He would make them respect him. He would have a name, a reputation, an identity. If he couldn't exceed them in stature, he would exceed them in power and wit.

So he faced his adversaries, he faced life, and he extracted from both everything they had to offer. He used his smile and generally good-natured temperament to win the confidence of the Romans and the deference of his countrymen. He was generous to those who favored him and paid well for service and loyalty.

He had everything he'd set out to get—and he reveled in his victory. On those nights when he wandered around in his empty house, he comforted himself with the recollection of the cleverness that had allowed him to build such a fine residence and appoint it with the best the empire had to offer. On those days when he walked the Jericho streets alone, and when people looked away and refused to greet him, he consoled himself with the thought that they all coveted his wealth and they all knew his name. Loneliness was a small price to pay for the distinction and privileges he enjoyed.

Zacchaeus frowned in frustration. Rare were the times when his distinction and privileges couldn't help him grasp the thing he wanted. This was one of those moments. If he'd had a little advance notice that this Jesus was coming, he could have bought himself a place along the street, but this unannounced visit robbed him of advantage.

Then he saw it: the tree. Opportunity! Oh, Zacchaeus, you are clever! Yes, that will do. After all, I don't want to speak to the Man; I just want to see Him. Zacchaeus looked around. He knew he'd have to hurry, and he couldn't run down the main street.

He darted along the side of the houses, raced to the sycamore tree, jumped, and heaved himself up onto its lowest branch. He secured his footing, slipped up along the trunk, pushed the leafy foliage aside, and looked for Jesus.

He wasn't any too soon. Just as he looked out across the crowd down the road, he saw Him—a slight-built man, surprisingly uncomely, not at all what he expected of one with so great a reputation. And He was laughing. Zacchaeus glanced around. What was so funny? Had someone fallen? Had a woman made a fool of herself? Had a child said something silly? The Man smiled and talked and stopped to bend and speak to the children who hugged His knees. The Man came closer, and Zacchaeus squatted down on his tree ledge to keep Jesus in sight.

Then Jesus stopped. He looked up, setting His eyes straight on Zacchaeus. Zacchaeus was so taken aback he stopped breathing. He couldn't move. He couldn't avert his eyes. The people around Jesus turned their heads to find out what Jesus was looking at. Everyone stared at Zacchaeus in silence. Zacchaeus had never had so much attention, and cold beads of sweat broke out on his forehead as he looked back at the smiling eyes of Jesus.

"Zacchaeus, hurry and come down; for I must stay at your house today."

His name—Jesus spoke his name. And He said it, not

with a disdainful spit, but with warm affection. Never had Zacchaeus heard his name spoken so.

"Yes, yes, yes, You may come to my house. Yes, oh yes, please do come." Zacchaeus scurried out of the tree and dropped to the ground to stand face-to-face with Jesus. He met those warm, name-speaking eyes, and as the good citizens of Jericho pouted and grumbled at the idea of Jesus in fellowship with such a sinner, Zacchaeus said, "Lord, half of my possessions I will give to the poor; and if I have defrauded anyone of anything, I will pay back four times as much." Jesus' face wrinkled with a radiating smile and while holding Zacchaeus' eager gaze, He cupped His hands on the short man's shoulders and said to the crowd, "Today salvation has come to this house, because this man, too, is a son of Abraham. For the Son of Man came to seek out and to save the lost.

"You have a name, Zacchaeus. You have a family, an identity, and a legacy. I claim you, Zacchaeus. You are found."

Jesus put His arm around Zacchaeus' shoulder, and they turned to walk together to a feast of fellowship and celebration.

• • • LUKE 19:1-10 • • •

Jesus entered Jericho and was passing through. A man was there by the name of Zacchaeus; he was a chief tax collector and was wealthy. He wanted to see who Jesus was, but being a short man he could not, because of the crowd. So he ran ahead and climbed a sycamore-fig tree to see him, since Jesus was coming that way.

When Jesus reached the spot, he looked up and

said to him, "Zacchaeus, come down immediately. I must stay at your house today." So he came down at once and welcomed him gladly.

All the people saw this and began to mutter, "He has gone to be the guest of a 'sinner.'"

But Zacchaeus stood up and said to the Lord, "Look, Lord! Here and now I give half of my possessions to the poor, and if I have cheated anybody out of anything, I will pay back four times the amount."

Jesus said to him, "Today salvation has come to this house, because this man, too, is a son of Abraham. For the Son of Man came to seek and to save what was lost" *(NIV)*.

8

Water Safe to Drink

JOHN 4:5-32

*S*he tried to focus her watery eyes as she walked down the dirt road. She'd tripped twice and almost lost the waterpot once because of her distraction. She cleared her eyes and cheeks of tears with the flat of her fingers, but they wouldn't stop coming. She had to get control of herself. What if someone saw her? Not that it was likely this time of day. The small houses were to her back, and the other villagers would keep to the shade of the walls and trees.

What was she going to do? The fights were more and more frequent, and if they couldn't be reconciled, what would become of her? He'd never threatened it, but she knew he could throw her out without notice. She worked hard to please him. Still—one could never be sure, never really relax. She'd learned that a very long time ago.

One couldn't be sure of much of anything—certainly not honor. It didn't matter how good you wanted to be—you had to accommodate. You had to compromise. You had to figure out what people wanted, what they needed from you, and, if you were going to survive, you had to provide what they wanted. Accommodation in exchange for acceptance was the way of life. If one didn't accommodate, one was abandoned. It was just that simple. And sometimes, like today, she wondered if the price of a roof and bread and an embrace wasn't too high. Sometimes she just wanted to walk away from it all and wander out into the wilderness and die. But she didn't. She stayed. And she kept trying to figure out how to make it all work.

She took a deep breath and looked up toward her destination. Oh, no. Someone was at the well. Oh, why today? Why today? *God, have You no mercy?* I need to be alone. I need time to think. And this time and place is all I have. Well, at least there will be silence. And maybe He'll move away when He sees me coming.

The Man had been leaning over the mouth of the well, trying to catch His reflection in the water below. He smiled at the silliness of the little game. The water was far too deep, and He couldn't really see anything except the shadow of His head blocking the light gray of the reflected sky. He straightened up, stretched His arms, and turned around to lean against the stones. Then He saw her: a woman walking toward the well, a woman with a waterpot, a woman with a tight face. He watched her.

The woman eyed the ground as she approached the well. She lifted the waterpot from her head and set it on the ground. She pulled out the drawing pot, and as she turned to drop it into the well, He spoke. She jumped. She looked sideways at His feet. Had her ears deceived her? Did He truly say, "Give Me a drink"? What did He want? Was He making a joke of her? Should she run? She stood sideways, drawing pot in her hands, lips pursed, eyes trying to take in as much of Him as she could and still avoid His face.

No, she wouldn't run. She'd had enough. She turned,

set the drawing pot on the stone ledge, and looked straight into His eyes and challenged, "How is it that You, being a Jew, ask me for a drink since I am a Samaritan woman?"

He met her eyes with a warm, friendly gaze and said in a gentle voice, "If you knew the gift of God, and who it is who says to you, 'Give Me a drink,' you would have asked Him, and He would have given you living water."

She nearly laughed but didn't. Her face relaxed. He sounded like a simpleton, but He wasn't. He wasn't anything like a simpleton. His words were strange, but His voice conveyed them with authority, and His eyes punctuated them with penetrating warmth. He was serious. He was sincerely offering her something.

She looked around Him for His drawing pot. "Sir," she responded softly, "You have nothing to draw with and the well is deep; where then do You get that living water? Jacob gave us this plentiful well. This water supplied him and his sons and his cattle. You are not greater than our father Jacob, are You?"

Jesus turned His body, leaned a little over the mouth of the well, and looked down. "Everyone who drinks of this water will thirst again, but whoever drinks of the water that I give shall never thirst; but instead, the water that I shall give shall become as a well of water springing up to eternal life."

Never thirst? Never have to draw again? A spring? A spring of never-ending, thirst-quenching water? What would this mean? What could be finer than such a possession? "Sir, give me this water so that I will not be thirsty, nor come all the way here to draw."

"Go, call your husband, and come here."

The catch. The trick. She should have known. She'd not be allowed to have such a gift all on her own. Well, she'd not share this with him, not, at least, until he apologized. And he's not my husband after all. She squared her shoulders, raised her chin, and said, "I have no husband."

"You have well said, 'I have no husband'; for you have had five husbands, and the one whom you now have is not your husband; you have spoken the truth."

She squinted at Him. Did she know this Man? Had He been in their village? She was sure she'd never seen Him before, and if a Jew had been in her village, she surely would have heard about it. How, then, did He know so much about her? Her eyes widened. This Man was a prophet—but a Jewish prophet. What did He have to do with Samaritans? What did He have to do with *her*? There was no place for Samaritans with the Jews!

"Sir, I perceive that You are a prophet. We worship, You know. We worship in this mountain, but you Jews don't accept that. You say Jerusalem is the only place where people can worship."

There! If He were a prophet, this Jew, let Him speak to His own people. She narrowed her eyes in defiance and waited for the slanderous rebuke.

The Man leaned forward, braced himself on His arm, and spoke in a quiet, confidential tone: "Woman, believe me, the time is coming when neither in this mountain, nor in Jerusalem, will people worship the Father. You worship that which you do not know; we Jews worship that which we *do* know, for salvation is from the Jews. But the time is coming, even now is at hand, when true worshipers shall worship the Father in spirit and truth. For you see, people who worship the Father in spirit and in truth are the kind of worshipers the Father seeks, for God is spirit, and those who worship Him must worship Him in spirit and truth."

Never had she heard anyone speak of God in such a way. This Man spoke as if He knew, really knew, God. And the way He spoke made her want to believe He was speaking the truth. A time was coming when worship wouldn't be confined to a place? As she studied His face and puzzled over His compelling words, a thought glanced across her mind: maybe He's talking about . . . she blurted, "I know that Messiah is coming, and when He comes, He will declare everything to us."

"I who speak to you am He."

This lonely, love-hungry, earthy woman stood face to face with the Holy Only Begotten. The Prince of Peace spoke words that stroked her ears with grace, wrapped her fears in comfort, and stamped the assurance of acceptance in her wounded heart. She didn't hear the voices behind her. She didn't remember about the clay pot. She looked at the genuinely happy face of the One who was smiling love at her, and she tasted the sweetness of the Living Water— the answer to her parched, famished soul.

A grace-drenched woman ran to tell an entire village of the One with living water.

• • •   JOHN 4:5-32   • • •

So he came to a town in Samaria called Sychar, near the plot of ground Jacob had given to his son Joseph. Jacob's well was there, and Jesus, tired as he was from the journey, sat down by the well. It was about the sixth hour.

When a Samaritan woman came to draw water, Jesus said to her, "Will you give me a drink?" (His disciples had gone into the town to buy food.)

The Samaritan woman said to him, "You are a Jew and I am a Samaritan woman. How can you ask me for a drink?" (For Jews do not associate with Samaritans.)

Jesus answered her, "If you knew the gift of God and who it is that asks you for a drink, you would have asked him and he would have given you living water."

"Sir," the woman said, "you have nothing to draw with and the well is deep. Where can you get this living water? Are you greater than our father Jacob, who gave us the well and drank from it himself, as did also his sons and his flocks and herds?"

Jesus answered, "Everyone who drinks this water will be thirsty again, but whoever drinks the water I give him will never thirst. Indeed, the water I give him will become in him a spring of water welling up to eternal life."

The woman said to him, "Sir, give me this water so that I won't get thirsty and have to keep coming here to draw water."

He told her, "Go, call your husband and come back."

"I have no husband," she replied.

Jesus said to her, "You are right when you say you have no husband. The fact is, you have had five husbands, and the man you now have is not your husband. What you have just said is quite true."

"Sir," the woman said, "I can see that you are a prophet. Our fathers worshiped on this mountain, but you Jews claim that the place where we must worship is in Jerusalem."

Jesus declared, "Believe me, woman, a time is coming when you will worship the Father neither on this mountain nor in Jerusalem. You Samaritans worship what you do not know; we worship what we do know, for salvation is from the Jews. Yet a time is coming and has now come when the true worshipers will worship the Father in spirit and truth, for they are the kind of worshipers the Father seeks. God is spirit, and his worshipers must worship in spirit and in truth."

The woman said, "I know that Messiah" (called Christ) "is coming. When he comes, he will explain everything to us."

Then Jesus declared, "I who speak to you am he."

Just then his disciples returned and were surprised to find him talking with a woman. But no one asked, "What do you want?" or "Why are you talking with her?"

Then, leaving her water jar, the woman went back to the town and said to the people, "Come, see a man who told me everything I ever did. Could this be the Christ?" They came out of the town and made their way toward him.

Meanwhile his disciples urged him, "Rabbi, eat something."

But he said to them, "I have food to eat that you know nothing about" *(NIV).*

9

The Break of Dawn; Morning Light

JOHN 18:17-18, 25-27; 21:11-13, 15-22

The Break of Dawn

"I do not know what you are talking about!"

The words were said before I thought.
The cold
the hunger
the crowd
the noise, the racket: in ceaseless murmur laden with
    threat.

I sought only brief comfort by the fire to burn the noise in
    its roar.
The words were stolen by a silly girl;

THE BREAK OF DAWN

They were said before I thought.
They will not be said again.
Next time she asks, I will tell her.

Restless bodies shift and slap,
Murmurs meet within the huddle—
"You are too one of them."

"No, no, man—I am not!"

Tiny, fierce lights from smudged faces blaze sight.
No one dims the light with motion.
They see my sweat.
They know my lie.
Will they kill me for the truth, or for the lie?
Better say the truth;
I'll own I'm His.

Large shadows with heaving arms and caves for teeth
    smother the air.
"Yes, yes—you are one of them!"

"No, no! May God rend me from head to heel if I know
    Him.
I do not know Him!"
Two eyes reach between the heads and, with heavy grace,
    meet mine.

Deaf. Empty. Suspended in humid silence
Then dropped, cut by a cock's crow.
Joints bent to ground by heavy bones,
Eyes punched by sticky fists,
Lap drenched with unreasoned tears—
Soul and heart laid bare to my merciless sight.

Morning Light

Breakfast finished, laughter full beside a warm fire.
Crumbs thrown into flames.
Fishbones brushed from hot stone.

"Peter, do you love Me more than these?"

Fire sears the bones,
Chars the crumbs.
A man shifts his weight.

"Lord, You know I love You."

Sand rubbed between hands,
Face turned to shadowed face.

"Peter, do you whole-heart love Me?"

The man measures his words to the motion of his hands.

"Lord, You know I love You."

Fire heats the stones,
Sea washes the sand, laps all sound.

"Peter, do you, then, half-heart love Me?"

A sound, hot from another fire, sears memory in the silence.
Eyes meet eyes,
Rushed breath forces whispered words.

"Lord, You know without my saying—
You know I love You."

"This I know, Peter, that when you are old,
you will be stretched, bound, and killed
for your whole-heart love of Me."

A step on stone.
Attention turns.

"What about him?"

"Peter, what is that to you?
You follow Me."

Then Jesus stood and walked away.

Meaning-filled spoken words;
Comprehended light fused a half-hearted soul.
Tears spotted the sand;
Breath heaved with release.
The envisioned was claimed.

A whole-hearted man rose and
followed Jesus.

• • • JOHN 18:17-18, 25-27; • • •
21:11-13, 15-22

The slave-girl therefore who kept the door said to Peter, "You are not also one of this man's disciples, are you?" He said, "I am not." Now the slaves and the officers were standing there, having made a charcoal fire, for it was cold and they were warming themselves; and Peter also was with them, standing and warming himself. . . . They said therefore to him, "You are not also one of His disciples, are you?" He denied it, and said, "I am not." One of the slaves of the high priest . . . said, "Did I not see you in the garden with Him?" Peter therefore denied it again; and immediately a cock crowed.

* * *

Simon Peter went up, and drew the net to land, full of large fish, a hundred and fifty-three; and although there were so many, the net was not torn. Jesus said to them, "Come and have breakfast." . . . Jesus came and took the bread, and gave them, and the fish likewise. . . . So when they had finished breakfast, Jesus said to Simon Peter, "Simon, son of John, do you love Me more than these?" He said to Him, "Yes, Lord; You know that I love You." He said to him, "Tend My lambs."

He said to him again a second time, "Simon, son of John, do you love Me?" "He said to Him, Yes, Lord; You know that I love You." He said to him, "Shepherd My sheep."

He said to him the third time, "Simon, son of John, do you love Me?" Peter was grieved because He said to him the third time, "Do you love Me?" And he said to Him, "Lord, You know all things; You know that I love You." Jesus said to him, "Tend My sheep. Truly, truly, I say to you, when you were younger, you used to gird yourself, and walk wherever you wished; but when you grow old, you will stretch out your hands, and someone else will gird you, and bring you where you do not wish to go." Now this He said, signifying by what kind of death he would glorify God. And when He had spoken this, He said to him, "Follow Me!"

Peter, turning around, saw the disciple whom Jesus loved following them; . . . Peter therefore seeing him said to Jesus, "Lord, and what about this man?" Jesus said to him, "If I want him to remain until I come, what is that to you? You follow Me!"